Poems from the vain heart of mine

Galileah Lomeli

Presentation by *BookLeaf Publishing*

Web: www.bookleafpub.com

E-mail: info@bookleafpub.com

ISBN: 9789357444576

First edition 2022

DEDICATION

To Ally and Sam, thank you for being my biggest cheerleaders. I love you and I thank you for the immense amount of support and love.

ACKNOWLEDGEMENT

How do I start? First off, I want to thank my closest friends for being so supportive and even more curious. Through them I found my love for writing again. Although I am young, I know many of us struggle with upholding our passions and running with it. I want to thank everyone who knew about this book, but was patient enough for the final product. I want to especially thank Ally and Sam, you two were my main cheerleaders through this all. I most certainly want to thank Bookleaf Publishing for helping make the journey in the completion of my poetry book smooth and enjoyable. I would not have been able to publish without them. And lastly, I would like to thank everyone who has helped me realize that writing is an outlet and art all in one.

Thank you!

PREFACE

Dear reader, first off I would like to thank you for choosing my poetry book today. In your hands you hold some of my work. These poems are thoughts scattered on what is now a physical outlet. They have meaning, so I thank you for choosing this book. These poems were all written in different settings, at different times. They share my outlook on life and the idea of it. This book contains words describing people I love, places that remind me of them, and the ones I have yet to find my way to. I want to thank you for taking the time to read this. To get to delve deep into my heart and find parts of me. I chose these poems out of all the poems I hold because they share parts of me I'm willing to discuss. I'm willing to let the reader see these words and digest them deeply and hopefully internalize them. There were many challenges along the way, as many writers face. But I am here to say that I did craft these poems through months of different thought processes and healing points. In the end, this book is a piece of me, and I hope you find either comfort or understanding in it.

Thank you!

Cold

A whisperer in the wind,
You called me like a siren at bay.
I wish I had ignored you,
And your wicked way.
The words you spoke luring me in,
Only to push me away.

unimaginative repetition

days and nights
crumpled tissues and internal fights
washed sweaters and shirts too tight
The suffocation of the screen
Our obscure dreams
Days and nights
And now we realize how
We are not different from
The moon and the sun

Suffocate me

In my chest
These moths of fear
Take over and I know that you are near

My knees shake like buildings in an earthquake
And my hands get cold
I hate this feeling
Your hands force my head underwater and I
cannot breathe

I fall to my knees at your feet and beg you to
leave,
But you invited yourself to live in my mind
Anxiety, you love to run me dry

Emotional nausea

I foolishly search for your validation,
In your eyes and your heart
I hope you have me on your mind
But even that feels far stretched

I pray to the moon,
That it watches over you
But I know very well
That you scream at the sun to scorch me

I want to call it love

I think about u too much
This obsession of infatuation has suffocated my
thoughts.
I think of you even when I know I shouldn't
Cupid's bow missed me,
Yet satan's greed cursed me.
I want to write about you always,
In a state of maddening hunger
And adoration.

I don't think you realize that the universe has its
plans
It's reasons and it's ways.
it knows your energy is winsome and desirable,
Far too complex and interesting for me.
Yet it likes to tease you and me,
As people and lovers.
It knows we shouldn't be together
But not once does it stop this union.
It's a game and we are blind
Hoping we catch what we should find.

Antithetical beings

I know they say opposites attract,
But it seemed as though we simply had nothing
to say
Our disconnected hearts reigned war
And it seemed as though even the thread of love
Could not keep us in tact
And no matter how well you knit it to the quilt
of our friendship
It was the lose string fate would pull and undo

Maybe we're doomed?

standing in the rain
As its drops caress your face like silk
It mimics the way I held you once.
I guess I am abjectly waiting
For you to come back.
I envy the rain now,
 As it mocks me by abrading my memories of
you.
I try to remember,
But your silence accosts me
And I forget you too.

Him

In this man
I see a beautiful gold soul.
He holds his head high
Yet he is kind and gentle.
His laugh lives in women's minds
But he isn't one to use or be used.
I wish he knew my intentions
And how much I admired him.

Nature's child

You are my pearl soul
 dancing in the field of flowers we claimed
And I fawn over you.
There's no music,
But the wind around you made an orchestrated
tune
Just so it could see you dance for a little longer.
I think the trees around you believe you are one
of them,
Because they too follow your movements.
The sun admires your beauty from above
And I think it is jealous of me,
Since it can only follow you so far.
But me? I will be with you till the moonlight
kisses you goodnight.

Home

I imagine you like a Victorian house
Tall and mysterious
Beautifully carved with detail
Charming and delicate

as the moonlight illuminates your features
And I think, how could anyone look away?
You believe me when I say this

Yet you see yourself as a shadow
A house that stands out too much and casts darkness
Dilapidated and cold
A place no one dares to step in and care for

The ocean's lover

The sand cowers at your feet,
The waves bow in your presence.
It's like you make an orchestra with the ocean,
A beautiful harmony in your favor.
And although your soul is attached to the city,
I know your heart belongs to the sea.

In harmony, California girl

The songs written about California girls
Could never amount to you.
My clock ticks when you breathe,
And my mouth curls into a smile.
The endless plans we made
And the hot air carries our laughs to our hearts.
My dearest coastal girl,
How I hate the beach
But I would take the sandy wind and cold salty water
Just because it reminds me of you, my California pearl.

Brooklyn babe

The shadow of your slick black hair,
Your eyes glistening with concentration.
I admire your passion
And the way the world rejoices your voice.
The Brooklyn born, California raised gem
I grew to be inspired by them.
And when you write,
 I know your New York soul is back.

New York, forever

I smile as you talk about your future.
I know you love the city of lights,
And just know, that even though we will be
apart,
my spirit dances in the hot summer nights with
you.
your feet sway on the train I long to be in
just so I can admire the look of NYC on you.
My little city girl, I'll miss you.

My little piece of Georgia

I never understood platonic lovers until you.
The feeling of an emotional mirror
Placed in two different states,
Bound to break.
I felt like you were the friend
I had asked the universe for
My little Georgia soul, so pretty,
like as if the gods had put a piece of their hearts
into mixing pots with pearls and sincerity.

Blocked

The artist in me wept and begged
To be let out of this cage
I had intentionally created
My hands held down by invisible strings and,
alas,
I had become a puppet to procrastination
The thought of incompetence fogged my brain
as daily as the blood in my veins
Oh, how I long for my artistic sanity.

The artist

We laughed with fogged minds and cold hands,
As we were reminded every time
we saw a movie
reflected on an art piece
or played a song
That no matter how long we stayed in our
sensitive minds,
The world would shun us and make us cower at
their feet.

We made the things that people apotheosized
and yet we were treated as if we had a plague
we had not yet understood ourselves.
In a sense we do.
A plague that ruled our mind,
This plague is called art.

Young Poet

My child brain,
Spinning with ideas and innocence
Saying so much yet nothing at all.
This belletristic mindset I grew fond of,
A curse and yet my own version of avidity.
Sitting in this empty, bright room
My hands, the lovers of my mind
Dancing in unison to speak words of truth
Or vanity.

Validation

I search for words that are not mine
In other's books and their weary looks
Chasing after perfection with splintered steps
Scars and bruises engraved into my soul
My mind encaged and tortured by false ideology
But at least now I'm just as good as they are.

Someone like you

Its strange
How much they compare me to you
It should be a compliment
But I just want to be me

yet it seems as though every time I did
something different
Your name was the first thing said
A melody to them
But to me it was a sound I should run from

I guess I shouldn't expect any better
I am merely a copy of you
A shadow you need, but don't want
How foolish, to think I'd be loved more
Just if I looked a little bit more like you.

The end

I dreamed about you being at the end of the
bridge
Smiling at me as I got closer
We never believed in heaven
But alas, here we were
And you stretched your hand out
Just like you would when I caught up
In those days when our curiosity for the natural
parts of the world
That led us into places our minds could not
create
Along the bridge we would stand and see the
water below
And we are back again in this dream of mine
And I was at peace
This was the end, my love.